D1741896

ADVENTURERS

ROUGH WATER CANOEING

Jeremy Evans

First published by Heinemann Children's Reference 1992, a division of Heinemann Educational Books Ltd, Halley Court, Jordan Hill, Oxford OX2 8EJ

OXFORD LONDON EDINBURGH
MADRID PARIS ATHENS BOLOGNA
MELBOURNE SYDNEY AUCKLAND SINGAPORE
TOKYO IBADAN NAIROBI GABORONE HARARE
PORTSMOUTH (USA)

Design by Julian Holland Publishing Ltd

Printed in Hong Kong

British Library Cataloguing in Publication Data

Evans, Jeremy
  Rough water canoeing. – (Adventurers)
  I. Title II. Series
  797.122

ISBN 0 431 00589 3

Acknowledgements
Illustrations: Rupert White Studio, Keith Chaffer, Martin Smillie.
Photographs: a = above, m = middle, b = below
All photographs were taken by the author except;
Cover, Pyranha (front), Pyranha (back), 5a, Pyranha; 6a, Pyranha; 10a, Pyranha; 31a, Pyranha; 32a, Pyranha; 38a, Pyranha; 40a, Pyranha; 41a, Pyranha; 42a, Bearsports Outdoor Centres; 43b, Alex Williams; 44b, Pyranha; 45a, Pyranha.

Thanks go to Mike Pickering of Pyranha for supplying so many excellent photos; to the paddlers of Woodmill Canoeing & Outdoor Activities Centre and the Holme Pierrepoint slalom course whose photos appear in this book; to John Handyside, Wild Water Senior Team Manager, for his help and advice; and to Trevor Bailey of the British Canoe Union, whose excellent BCU Canoeing Handbook provides an unrivalled wealth of information on paddling.

Note to the reader
In this book there are some words in the text which are printed in **bold** type. This shows that the word is listed in the glossary on page 46. The glossary gives a brief explanation of words which may be new to you.

Contents

Origins of the canoe

Dressed for a fun paddle in a modern version of the Native American canoe.

No one knows when the first canoe appeared. It almost certainly developed from people sitting astride logs and paddling them to cross open stretches of water. The next stage would have been to tie logs together and use them as a raft. The dug-out, made by hollowing out a log and sharpening the ends, provided a faster means of transport and is still widely used in some parts of the world.

The dug-out gave room to kneel or squat inside, but was both heavy and restricted in shape. Native Americans developed light timber framed canoes, using buffalo skin or birch bark for the outer coverings to keep the water out. They knelt and propelled the boat with a single bladed paddle.

The first kayaks

The original Inuit (Eskimo) **kayaks** were made with seal skins stretched over a frame made of bone or driftwood. The kayak is what is usually referred to as a canoe. It is used with a double-ended paddle.

The adoption of the kayak

With its covered deck, small cockpit and double ended paddle, the kayak was originally developed for crossing icy seas and for hunting and fishing.

Kayaks were adopted for leisure use by the Victorians. The most famous was John MacGregor's Rob Roy, built in 1865, which enabled this gentleman explorer to cover 1000 miles of European waterways. Its successor, Rob Roy II, journeyed as far as Jordan and the Nile. It is displayed in the British National Maritime Museum in London. John MacGregor's exploits were described in a number of books, and made this new sport so popular that the world's first Canoe Club was founded on the River Thames at Twickenham, England in 1866. It became the Royal Canoe Club in 1873. The kayak is widely used in Europe today, although in America the **Canadian canoe** remains popular.

Canoe v kayak

The open deck of the Canadian canoe offers much more storage and space than a kayak, and is therefore more suitable for touring. For camping trips it can be inverted to form a shelter on dry land. It is less suitable for open sea use though, since the open deck can become swamped by the waves. However, **closed cell foam** in the bottom of the boat should provide sufficient **buoyancy** to turn it upright if it capsizes.

With its double ended paddle and closed deck a kayak is more manoeuvrable than a Canadian canoe. It also performs better in rough water. The skills needed to handle either well are similar.

The techniques described in this book refer most often to the kayak.

Different shapes and sizes

Short, highly manoeuvrable kayaks are best for white water fun.

The performance of a canoe or kayak is affected by its length, its width, its volume, its weight and its bottom shape. Other factors such as **rocker line,** which is the amount of curve along the bottom from nose to tail, need to be taken into account according to what it will be used for. Thus we have different shaped and sized canoes for learning, touring, all round fun, open sea use, stunts and freestyle. Competition canoeing includes **slalom** and **white water** racing which, with **wild water,** covers all rough water use.

Bottom shapes

The bottom shape of the canoe changes along its length. The rounded shape gives very poor **directional stability,** but combined with a high level of rocker it allows the canoe to be turned very easily. A vee shape gives excellent directional stability, but, with a flat rocker line, makes the canoe slow to turn.

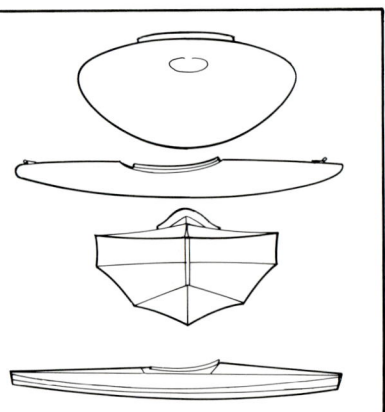

Types of canoes

A touring canoe needs a high level of directional stability for covering long distances. It is around 440cms long, at least 60cms wide, has a shallow vee-shaped bottom, and a flat rocker line.

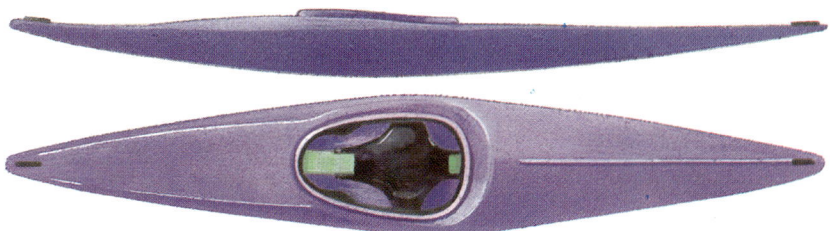

A slalom canoe must be quick and agile to allow a rapid increase of speed. A typical example is quite short (around 360cms), with a rounded bottom, acute rocker line and a lack of volume or low buoyancy.

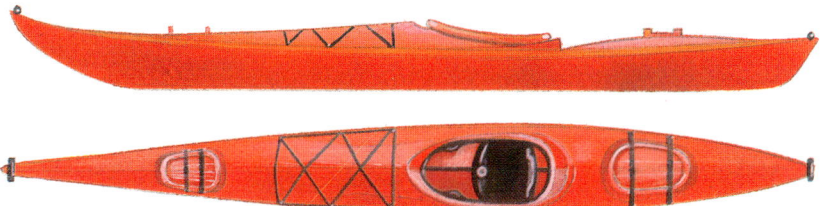

A sea touring canoe is closest to the original Inuit kayak. It is over 500cms long and comparatively narrow (60cms or less), with a straight keel and flared sides on a rounded vee-shaped hull.

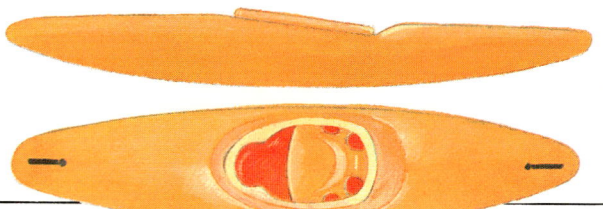

A white water play boat is only around 330cms long with high **volume** and a high rocker line.

What canoes are made of

The majority of today's canoes are made of plastic. The cheapest and most popular material is **roto** or **blow moulded polyethylene.** This is cheap to build in, reasonably light, and very durable for the type of action shown here. It does not need too much care either.

For more high performance boats, glass-reinforced plastic, using exotic materials such as **kevlar** and carbon, is preferred, as it can produce a much lighter, stiffer boat. A top slalom or wild water boat built in these exotic plastics may cost up to three times as much as the polyethylene version. It is also much more fragile, suffers from knocks, and needs constant repair and care. Wood construction is occasionally used for sprint racing canoes.

Choosing paddles

Kayaks are controlled with a doubled-ended paddle and Canadian canoes with a single blade. To find the right length for a double ended paddle, you should be able to curl your hand over the top blade. Paddle shafts can be made of aluminium, wood or fibreglass, and the blades of wood, fibreglass, **ABS plastic,** or a combination of carbon and glass. The blade shapes are either flat, curved or spooned, with the blades usually set at right angles.

Parts of a kayak

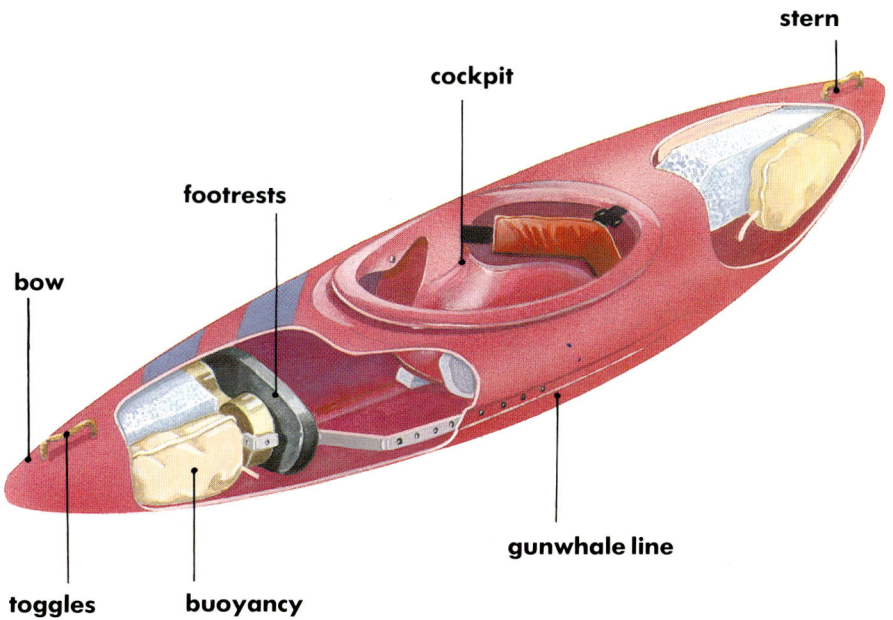

stern

cockpit

footrests

bow

gunwhale line

toggles   buoyancy

BUOYANCY A canoe should have at least 25kg of **positive buoyancy** to ensure it will float when swamped. Most manufacturers use a **buoyancy block** of rigid **ethafoam** at both **bow** and **stern**.

COCKPIT The cockpit has a small seat set towards the back. The lip round its edge is called the **coaming**, and can be used to hold a spraydeck.

FOOTRESTS These hold your feet rigidly in position. This is particularly important when you're in white water. In the event of a collision, you should be able to keep your position without sliding down.

TOGGLES Both bow and stern of the canoe should have a toggle, end loop, or handle to provide a handhold. Toggles are the best for white water use as they are safer to grab hold of.

Safety first

● On fibreglass canoes, check the bottom and where the hull is joined for leaks.

● Check that the canoe will float evenly when swamped or capsized. The buoyancy blocks must be securely fixed.

● The footrest should be rigid but adjustable. If your feet are forced beyond it, you must be able to withdraw them.

● Don't use end loops in fast moving water. If the canoe capsizes they could twist around your fingers and give you a serious injury.

9

Safety equipment

Canoeists should always wear buoyancy whatever the conditions. In white water and surf this is especially important however expert the paddler. Even with a very stable canoe, something may cause it to capsize when you are least prepared. You need buoyancy that will help you get to the surface quickly, and help you stay afloat while you sort out your problems.

In white water there is also a very real danger of head injury and a safety helmet designed for canoeing should be worn. Most of these have a foam inner lining with a hard plastic outer shell.

Buoyancy aids

Most canoeists favour a **buoyancy aid** rather than a **lifejacket.** Buoyancy aids must have at least 6kg of positive buoyancy to conform to International Canoe Federation regulations for competition. They are shaped like waistcoats, usually with zip front or fitting over the head. Different styles are available for different kinds of watersports. Apart from a good tight fit which won't ride up over your body the buoyancy aid needs to be cut freely round the shoulder so that your arms have plenty of freedom of movement for paddling.

Lifejackets

A lifejacket is more bulky than a buoyancy aid but it will support your head or keep your mouth and nose out of the water in the unlikely event of your being knocked unconscious. For white water paddling some canoeists favour the least bulky types of lifejackets, which have two stages of buoyancy. In normal use they provide the minimum 6kg of a buoyancy aid, while the optional inflatable collar transforms them into a full lifejacket. Remember that a lifejacket is only a safety aid. It is up to you to judge the conditions.

What to wear

What you wear for canoeing depends on the time of year, the temperature of both air and water, how long you intend staying on the water, and whether you're going to get wet. Canoeing can be a strenuous pastime which warms you up, but the chilling effect of cold water should never be forgotten. Your body loses heat 26 times faster in water than it does in air at the same temperature. All cold water canoeists should wear a neoprene wetsuit as the basis of their clothing, with additional layers that can be added or removed as necessary.

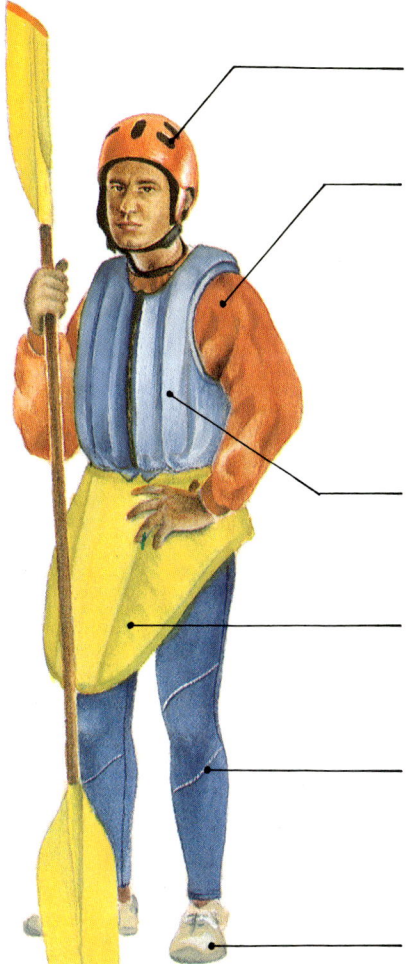

A crash helmet is necessary for white water or surf.

A dry top with neck and wrist seals keeps water out in very cold weather.

An anorak or cagoule is worn for less cold conditions.

Thermal underwear is useful in cold weather.

A buoyancy aid keeps you safe.

Gloves are not usually worn as you need to feel the paddles.

The spraydeck is worn around your waist and is fitted to the cockpit coaming to keep the canoe dry.

The long-john or shortie style neoprene wetsuit covers the lower body and chest. In warm weather shorts may be adequate.

Neoprene boots are worn for cold weather, trainers for warmer weather.

Canoeing safely

The basic rules for safe canoeing are: You should be able to swim confidently, and cope with being in or under the water. However well you can swim, a buoyancy aid or lifejacket should be worn.

If your canoe capsizes, stay with it. The canoe will float and provide something for you to cling to, and is easily spotted on the water. There are exceptions to this rule. For instance, if the current is carrying you and the canoe into danger, you may need to abandon it and make for the shore. If you do this, always inform the relevant authorities that you are safe.

Always canoe in company. The ideal number for a canoeing expedition is at least three trained paddlers who should be able to cope with most situations if they have sufficient experience.

Danger of hypothermia

Hypothermia is a condition in which the body temperature becomes dangerously low. The cause is exhaustion together with exposure to cold, particularly to cold water. It is prevented by wearing the right clothing, and recognizing the symptoms. These start with your skin turning pale, followed by shivering. This is a sign for you to get off the water and warm yourself up. If you don't the condition can get rapidly worse, leading to impaired judgement, clumsy movement and apathy. In extreme cases final stages are unconsciousness and death.

Starting out in a canoe

Canoeing is by no means as simple as it appears. Racing, slalom and wild water canoes need expert handling. This is only learnt with practice, experience, and expert tuition. Courses are widely available in many countries. The addresses of the principal national bodies which control them are given on page 46.

Getting into a kayak demands care. Hold it alongside the bank or jetty. Step in with one foot first, then support your weight on the opposite hand, as you get in.

Sit down on the back of the cockpit, and then push your legs down towards the bow, slipping down onto the seat as you do so. Reverse this procedure for getting out.

Your first canoeing expedition should take place on calm water, which is known as placid water. This generally means on lakes, ponds, reservoirs and rivers. A stable, touring canoe is the easiest to learn on. To start with, accessories such as spraydecks, which require extra skill in a capsize, are best avoided.

In a more advanced launch, the kayak is rocked until it falls into the water.

This is a sideways launch. The same technique can be used forwards.

Paddling

Trying out the effects of basic paddling and control strokes on a placid river.

Paddling is a skill which relies on a series of different strokes which can be linked to propel the canoe to maximum effect. Some of these strokes are basic, others are more advanced.

Basic control strokes for starting, moving forwards, stopping or turning the canoe include forward and reverse paddling; stopping; **forward** and **reverse sweep strokes; draw strokes;** and **recovery strokes.**

More advanced strokes for turning and steering the canoe include the **stern rudder; low brace turn;** and **bow rudder.** There are also **sculling** strokes which are advanced versions of the basic draw stroke and recovery stroke, the **sculling draw** and **sculling for support,** shown on pages 20 and 21.

Safety first

● Check that the footrest is adjusted so that you have a comfortable and secure paddling position, with your knees braced against the sides of the boat. This allows you to paddle freely with your lower body rigid.
● Make sure the paddle is the right length for you. Shorter shafts are preferred for better control in white water.
● Your clothing should not restrict your movement. You should be able to turn the top half of your body and lean forwards or back.

Forward and reverse paddling

A canoeist has to develop the feel of paddling. In a kayak, with the blades angled at 90 degrees to each other, one hand acts as the control hand which always grips the paddle, while the other lets the shaft rotate.

In normal position hands are evenly spaced on the paddle shaft.

The forward stroke propels the canoe. It is a **high stroke,** in which the paddle blade is pulled through the water as close to the boat as possible.

With each stroke the body twists as the control blade drops into the water as far forward as possible. The blade is pulled back until the other arm is straight.

In a round-bottomed kayak, the forward stroke can be surprisingly difficult to perform properly. Normal faults include not keeping the blades close enough to the sides of the boat which makes it start turning, not putting them into the water at the same angle, which leads to an uneven course, and watching the paddle rather than looking ahead.

REVERSE STROKES

These are important for stopping or for reversing out of difficulties. A **low stroke,** with the blade well away from the sides of the canoe, is used for reverse steering. A high stroke, with the blades close to the canoe, is used for power when reversing in a straight line. If you are being carried forward at speed, do not try to reverse suddenly at full power.

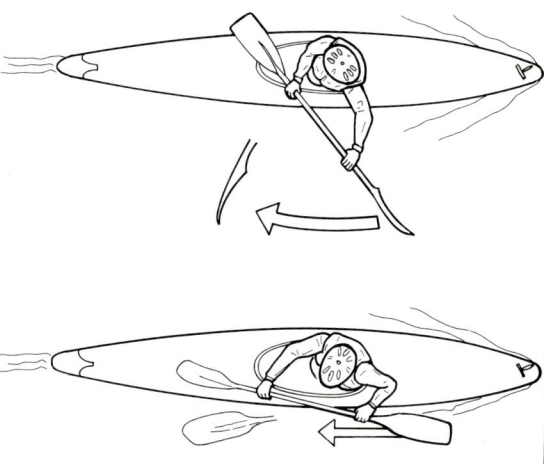

More basic control strokes

Bringing the blade down for a high recovery stroke to stabilise the kayak.

Other basic strokes can be used to steady a canoe if it tips over; to turn it quickly and powerfully; or to move it sideways through the water.

The recovery stroke steadies the canoe when it is in danger of capsizing. Push the back of the blade hard down against the water on the side the canoe is tipping.

The sweep stroke is a low stroke used to turn the canoe. It can be performed forwards or backwards. Beginners can use it for correcting turns caused by poor technique.

The draw stroke is a high stroke which pulls the canoe sideways through the water – for instance if you want to move alongside a river bank or another canoeist sideways through the water. These must be mastered before moving on.

Recovery strokes

The recovery stroke should be used as soon as you feel the canoe is tipping into a capsize. If you reach out far enough, and bring the back of the blade hard down onto the water fast enough, it will give you a short time in which to recover your balance. At the same time you must lift your knees up against the top side of the canoe and roll your hips to help bring the canoe level.

The **high recovery stroke** allows an experienced canoeist to recover from extreme angles in rough water. A **low recovery** can be used to hold a canoe steady.

Sweep strokes

With the blade at right angles to the surface of the water, the paddle is pulled in a wide sweep through it to finish at the back of the canoe. The control arm is kept completely straight.

The sweep stroke is a powerful turning stroke when done properly. Problems can arise from not sweeping in a wide enough arc, not using all of the blade, or not turning the body to help the stroke. Jamming the blade under the stern can result in a capsize.

Draw strokes

With the draw stroke the body is turned sideways and the control blade is dropped into the water as far from the canoe as possible. Drawing the flat surface of the blade smartly inwards will pull the canoe towards it. The canoeist pushes his or her knees up against the top side of the canoe. For all these strokes the canoeist should look ahead, not at the paddle.

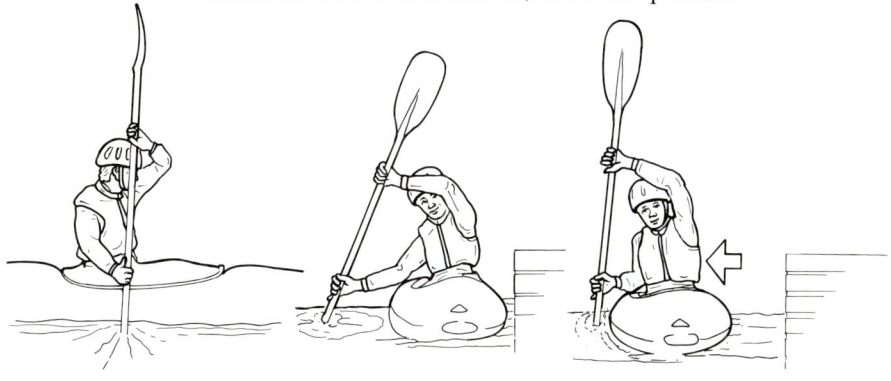

Water speed

More advanced turns rely on water speed, so are most effective when carried out in moving water. If you paddle on a lake or reservoir there will probably be no current, so your speed through the water, which is called water speed, is the same as your speed would be over ground, which is called ground speed. If you paddle on a river it will be moving, either with you or against you. Thus if you paddled at 5kph water speed, with a current flowing at 1kph, your ground speed would be 6kph. If you paddled against the same current at 5kph, your ground speed would be 4kph. If you didn't paddle at all your water speed would be nil, and your ground speed would be 1kph, either forwards or backwards.

Dangers in moving waters

The moving water of a current is very powerful. If a canoe collides with a fixed object such as a moored boat, rock, or tree, the current can pin the canoe or canoeist against it. The most dangerous obstacles of all are man-made weirs, which are built to divert or control the flow of a river. These create **stoppers** of circulating water which can trap a canoe and hold the canoeist underwater, despite wearing buoyancy. The way a stopper works is shown on page 29.

Advanced turns

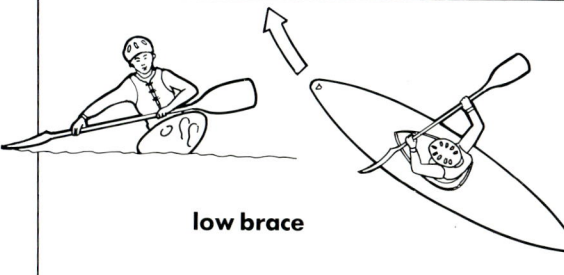

low brace

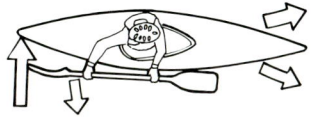

stern rudder

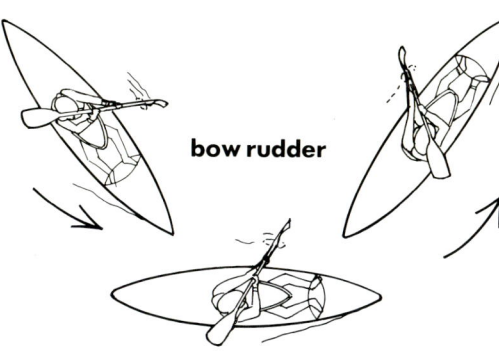

bow rudder

Canoe questions

Q: What is the difference between **leaning** and **edging**?
A: Leaning is angling the body inwards as you do when cycling. Edging is setting the canoe onto its side by angling your hips and lifting the knee and thigh against the upper side of the canoe.

LOW BRACE
This is a slow, safe turn which you can use on moving water.

As you go forwards edge the kayak onto its side by lifting either the right or left knee hard up against the top side of the kayak. This has the effect of altering the bottom shape in the water so that it starts a long wide turn. The back of the inside paddle blade is held out flat on the water, so that it skids across the surface.

STERN RUDDER
In this turn, the blade is trailed through the water and acts like a rudder as the canoe moves. This gives a fine control of turns.

Pushing the blade away from the boat on its left hand side turns it to the left. Pulling the blade inwards turns it right.

BOW RUDDER
This is the most dynamic turning stroke of all and is the quickest in white water.

The bow is pushed round by planting the blade with a high stroke, bracing your top arm across your forehead, and pulling the blade forward. The paddler's knees and feet help to push the kayak through the turn.

Sculling strokes

Sculling is moving the working blade back and fore, angling it at the end of each stroke so that its **leading edge** is pointing away from the boat. The blade is sliced through the water in a smooth rhythm, using the lower arm and both wrists. As with all paddling techniques you need to have control of the paddle without looking at it. This is called paddle awareness.

The power of the sculling stroke has the effect of drawing the canoe sideways. It can be used for sculling for support, (known as the **sculling brace**). It is useful when a recovery stroke isn't enough to prevent a capsize when the canoe is forced onto its edge.

Sculling for support

While the canoe is tipped on its side, perhaps due to the action of a wave or the wind pushing it over, the paddler will have to scull for support if the blade sinks before a hip flick can be used to bring the canoe back upright. The paddler pulls the blades sideways back and forth through the water with the leading edge lifted. At the same time he uses his knee on the sculling side to push the canoe out of the capsize, with thighs and hips helping to correct the angle.

Sculling draw

The sculling draw is an extension of the basic draw stroke. It pulls the canoe sideways through the water. The working blade is sculled back and fore and **feathered** at the end of each stroke to create the necessary pull. The paddle is held higher than for sculling support so that the blade can be kept close in by the side of the canoe. At the mid-point of each stroke, it is held upright. Note that the paddler twists his body to look in the direction of **sideslip.**

Hanging brace

brace with paddle   hip flick straightens kayak

The hanging or high brace is a support stroke used to steady the canoe when it is held in fast moving water, such as in a stopper. A hanging brace uses the front of the blade, while a low brace uses the back of the blade. Both can be adapted as sculling strokes as necessary.

Basic capsize practice

In a swimming pool

You can enjoy yourself without capsizing a kayak, but you need to learn to capsize before you go on to more advanced techniques. You should learn how to control a capsize before it happens in earnest. The best and warmest place to learn is in the controlled environment of a swimming pool with expert help on hand. Although this is going to be very different from a sudden capsize in white water or surf, at least you will have practised the various techniques.

A controlled capsize

You can capsize a kayak by sitting in the boat, gripping the sides with your knees, and leaning forward with your arms round the side of the boat. As you roll the kayak to the upside-down position bang the bottom three times with your hands, to show that you are in control.

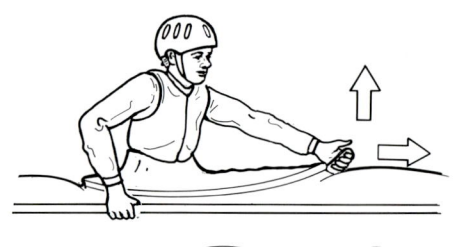

If you are using a spraydeck, you need to release it from the cockpit coaming before you can get out.

Coming out under control

Hold the cockpit coaming with both hands and push the canoe upwards. Release the grip of your knees and lean further forwards. This will push you into a forward somersault out of the cockpit. When you come to the surface grab hold of the boat. Swim to the front.

Recovering the canoe

Once you're at the front, rest the bow on your shoulder and swim the kayak into shallow water or take it ashore. It's easiest to empty out the water if there is a person at each end. If it is full, take care to pour out the water gradually, or you may risk damaging a fragile boat. Finally, raise and lower the ends to get rid of all the water. If you have to empty a kayak alone, the easiest method is to hold one end and rest the other on a higher level, for instance at the top of a sloping river bank.

Safety first

● Practise capsize drill regularly so that you know what to expect.
● When a kayak has capsized, always exit with a forward somersault. If you try to slide out backwards, it's possible to jam your legs in the cockpit and bruise your thighs as you struggle to get free.
● Don't attempt to right a kayak by yourself until you have reached shallow water.

Deep water rescues

If you're not able to pull your kayak into shallow water after a capsize you can get another canoeist to help you without going ashore. This is known as deep water rescue. Whatever you do, you must get a firm handhold on the boat as soon as you escape from the capsize, and pick up the paddle if you have dropped it.

Despite the name, deep water rescues can be used in quite shallow water. They should be avoided in breaking surf, where it is safest to tow the capsized boat and paddler out of the danger area. There are many different methods of rescue such as the **X rescue** and **HI rescue,** involving two or more other canoeists. Like most rescue techniques these are best learnt in a swimming pool with expert supervision.

Safety first

● In cold weather, get the capsized canoeist out of the water as quickly as possible to avoid hypothermia.
● Practise deep water rescues. Time these sessions to see how long a rescue may take.
● Modify your rescue technique to suit the situation.
● Learn how to give **expired air resuscitation.** This can be done in the water, using the bow of your canoe for support, or across the decks of two rafted canoes.

The X rescue

The X rescue enables one rescuer to recover and empty a capsized kayak without help other than from the capsized canoeist. First, the capsized kayak is pulled across the upright kayak's foredeck. This must be done quickly so that it doesn't fill up with too much water. It can then be rocked back and forth to empty the water. The capsized canoeist can help with this. Once empty, it is turned the right way up and lowered into the water. Using both boats as a support, the capsized canoeist can lift his feet into the cockpit while floating on his back, and then climb in.

The rescuer paddles up to the capsized boat.

He then quickly pulls it across the foredeck of his own boat to empty out the water.

He turns it the right way up and launches it alongside his own boat.

A paddle held across the two canoes can make getting back in easier.

The HI rescue

The HI rescue involves two rescuers. They make a raft of their canoes facing the capsized boat, and lift one end of it onto a paddle linking them. The capsized canoeist can hold the other end and rock the boat until it is empty. The rescuers then right it, enabling the capsized canoeist to crawl up over the stern.

Kayak rolls

Kayak rolls were developed by the Inuit who needed to be able to right their capsized kayaks quickly in freezing seas. Rolling is only possible when a spraydeck has been fitted. The technique is best learnt under supervision in a swimming pool, where such problems as disorientation, getting water up your nose, too much buoyancy in your clothing for easy movement underwater, and mastering the **hip-flick** can be easily overcome.

There are a number of different techniques which allow you to roll easily and keep your paddle at all times. These include the **pawlata roll**, the **screw roll**, the **reverse screw roll**, the **steyr roll**, the **hand roll**, the **storm roll** and the **vertical paddle roll**. The pawlata is considered the easiest roll to start with.

Safety first

● Before attempting rolls, be sure you can get out of the kayak with the spraydeck fitted.
● Learn to swim with the kayak on its side, holding it with the lower part of your body. Grip the capsized kayak with your knees, and let your upper body float to the surface by bending back and turning to one side. Using the breast stroke and pushing down with your hands, you can pull the canoe along behind you, though it's hard work.

Hip flicks and rolls

The hip flick rolls the kayak upright. You pull up with one knee and push down with the other. It should be completed in one quick movement. As soon as the flick is completed you sit upright. It is most easily learned in a swimming pool because you can practise flicking the canoe up with your hips, hanging on to the edge with both hands.

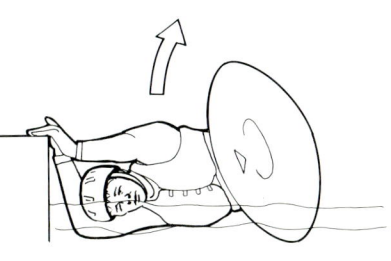

In the pawlata roll the paddle is held alongside the kayak, one hand gripping the middle while the other grips the blade further back. In the screw roll the technique is much the same but the paddle is held closer to its normal position. In most rolls the canoeist leans forward in the cockpit as the kayak capsizes. When the rear blade of the paddle breaks the surface, a sweep stroke through the water with the other blade allows the canoeist to hip flick upright.

The upside down stage of a reverse screw roll. It is termed reverse, because the paddler leans backwards rather than forwards.

The paddle is pushed out to one side prior to the hip flick which will bring the kayak back upright. All this happens very quickly.

With less leverage than in a pawlata roll, a more pronounced hip flick is required.

The kayak completes its roll, as the paddler comes up for air on its successful completion.

Calm water canoeing

Good behaviour

When canoeing on rivers and inland waters:
- Get permission if required.
- Avoid damaging banks and vegetation.
- Avoid disturbing fish or wildfowl.
- Paddle a careful course past fishermen.
- Keep in single file in a group on narrow waterways.
- Don't be noisy
- Make sure you can be easily spotted by larger craft.
- If in doubt, give way. Larger craft are less manoeuvrable.
- Give way to competition canoeists.
- Respect less experienced canoeists.
- Only come ashore at proper places.
- Dispose of litter correctly.

Safety first

- Always wear buoyancy.
- Check the weather and local conditions.
- Check if you can pass through tunnels. Take a light and a whistle so that other craft can see and hear you.
- Carry your canoe round locks.
- Keep away from weirs, sluices and fast flowing water.
- If you see any signs of pollution in the water, contact the local authorities.
- Inland waters have micro-organisms present. Where possible avoid swallowing the water and cover any cuts.

Calm water dangers

Danger ahead! Going from calm water to the white water beyond a weir.

Skilled canoeists can shoot weirs, waterfalls and stoppers but if you are learning you should never go over a weir you don't know. If in doubt, carry your canoe round it. The weir acts like a waterfall, with the water falling rapidly over a drop. At the bottom it swirls round in a circular motion which is called a stopper. This tends to trap anything that gets into it.

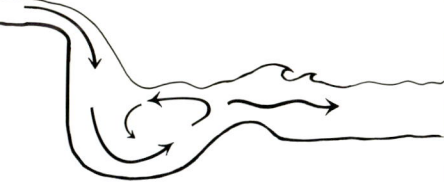

The violent backtow set up by a severe stopper may make escape impossible.

Throw ropes

Throw bags or throw ropes are carried by many canoeists. They can be thrown to rescue someone from a stopper, or other difficulties. The rope must float, it must be thick enough for an easy handhold, and it must be long enough to reach. The recommended length is 15-25 metres.

Hold the free end, and throw the bag.

29

Reading the water

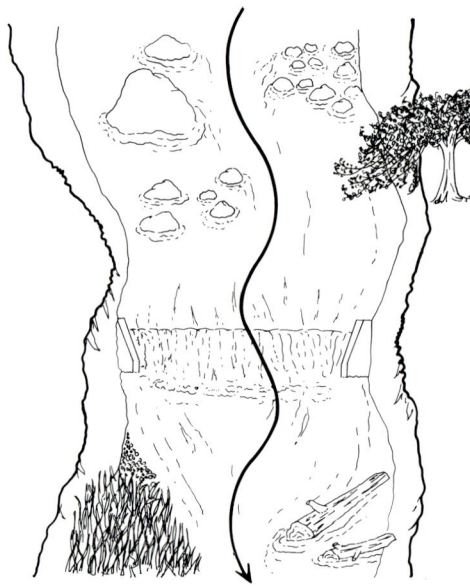

Being able to read the water is one of the main skills of more advanced canoeing. It is vital when you're paddling through wild water caused by rapids or falls. If the river has no obstructions the water generally flows fastest in the middle where there is least drag, and slowest at the sides. If you're paddling upstream, then you should keep to the sides whenever you can. If you are paddling across the river towards a far shore, take care that the faster water does not push the stern of your canoe round, making you **broadside** to the current.

Bends in the river

On a river bend, the deep water is on the outside of the bend, so the fastest flow will be there. The water on the inside where it is shallowest slows right down.

On a sharp bend the fast-flowing water hits the bank ahead of it and creates an area of turbulent water where the currents can be very confused. How severe this is depends on the speed and depth of the water, and the shape of the bank. An experienced paddler learns when to take action to avoid being swept into this rough area which may swamp his canoe and pinion it.

Grades of difficulty

Rivers are graded according to their difficulty. The grades are merely guidelines, as conditions can change dramatically. When the level of the water is high due to heavy rain or melting snow, the river will move at its fastest (in full spate). When it is low, due maybe to a long summer drought, it will move more slowly. Rocks and shallows may pose different problems. The difficulty will also depend on how experienced you are. A river that is difficult for one paddler may be easy for someone else. Choosing the right equipment is important. A wild water kayak can perform better in rapids than a general purpose touring kayak.

GRADE 1 Not difficult. Regular stream and waves, small rapids, simple obstructions.
GRADE 2 Moderately difficult. Irregular stream and waves, medium rapids, simple obstructions, small drops.
GRADE 3 Difficult. High irregular waves, larger rapids, stoppers, eddies, whirlpools, boulders, drops, numerous obstructions.
GRADE 4 Very difficult. Must be inspected. Continuous rapids, heavy stoppers, whirlpools, pressure areas, big boulders obstructing the stream, undertow.
GRADE 5 Extremely difficult. Inspection essential. Extreme rapids, stoppers, whirlpools, pressure areas, narrow passages, steep gradients and drops. Difficult access and landing.
GRADE 6 Practically impossible.

A Grade 5 river poses extreme difficulties, and may become Grade 6 in flood conditions.

Wild water falls and rapids

Most rivers have falls and rapids along their length. Waterfalls are caused by a sudden drop in the river and may be vertical. By taking care to avoid the shallow edge before the drop, canoes can get past small falls safely. Experts can even canoe over big falls as shown in the photograph.

Rapids are an area of fast moving water squeezed through a narrow gap, such as a gorge or canyon, or where the river suddenly becomes shallow. This creates waves which form lines across the river. The wild water created by the rapids sweeps you along with it. To get through them you have to go fast and steer well. Rocks have to be avoided. The canoe has to be paddled so that the water flows around it, and doesn't control it, leaving the paddler free to manoeuvre.

Rocks and eddies

Rocks cause disturbances in moving water. A rock just below the surface in slow water will set up a small wave just behind it. In deeper, faster water the wave will be larger. Big rocks can also create stoppers of circulating white water, in the same way as weirs do, as described on page 29. Fast paddling, using all the power you have, will help you to get safely past. By contrast, eddies are areas of still water beyond rocks. An eddy is created when water flows round and past a big rock sticking above the surface, rather than over the top of it. When you're paddling in rapids an eddy is a good place to stop from the perils of waves and stoppers. You can rest and plan the next move, using some of the techniques explained on page 34.

Wild water competition

Going full speed into a stopper in a wild water competition.

Wild water competition involves racing through rapids, and is a test of strength, speed, endurance and flexibility. Rivers of Grade 4 or 5 difficulty are used. The races may last up to 30 minutes over a course of at least three kilometres. The competitors set off down the course one by one, choosing a route that is as free of rocks as possible and using the best combination of boat and current speed that they can.

There is racing for all standards of canoeists. A World Championship held every second year attracts around 18 nations. In 1991 the championship was held in Bovec in Yugoslavia. The 1995 Junior World Championship venue is Bala in Wales, U.K. A World Cup series of seven major international races is held annually.

Safety first

● Always canoe in company in fast moving water and rapids. There should never be less than three of you!

● Wherever you can, check out an unfamiliar stretch of river from the land before going on the water.

● A helmet and closely fitting buoyancy aid or lifejacket are vital when paddling through rapids and rocks. The footrest must be properly adjusted and the boat must have enough buoyancy.

● Techniques such as the **ferry glide, break in** and **break out** must be mastered.

Wild water techniques

Edging the kayak to cross the stream, with the paddle acting as a brace.

Break out and break in

The break out is used for getting out of the main current into an eddy. The technique is to steer your bow into an eddy immediately downstream of the obstruction in the river that is causing it. When the bow is stopped by the eddy, the stern will be swept round by the main flow so that the canoe is fully in the eddy.

The break in is to get you out of the eddy. You paddle up to the obstruction, and push your bow into the main stream with a forward sweep stroke. As your stern is held by the eddy, the bow will be pushed downstream.

Edging and ferry glides

Your kayak should be kept level when you're paddling directly downstream or upstream. When you are paddling across the stream it must be edged. This means leaning downstream to raise the upstream side. This prevents water pressure against the deck from capsizing you.

An important technique for crossing a stream is the ferry glide. This stops you losing ground by being swept downstream and you can manoeuvre the boat without getting swept onto rocks. The principle is to set a course angle which allows for sideslip.

White water rafting

White water rafting is a popular paddling alternative. Many of the great wild water rivers of the world have specialist companies offering raft trips, using inflatable neoprene boats that ride down the rapids. These rafts can carry as many as 12 people with equipment and provisions for a week long tour, or be a simple one or two person raft.

Wild water rafting is potentially dangerous. Rafts can capsize and there have been fatalities, so it goes without saying that those in charge of the big rafting trips must be highly experienced, since everyone's safety relies on their skill and judgement. The rafts are paddled on either side. On the bigger rafts, a helmsperson sits at the back, steering with a paddle and shouting instructions to the paddlers.

Breaking records

- Ray Hudspith, from the UK, completed 1000 kayak rolls in 35 minutes in 1987.
- Sweden's Gert Fredriksson won six Olympic gold medals between 1948 and 1960, as well as 13 world titles.
- The Internation Long River Canoeists Club's Rhine Challenge is over a 714 mile (1149km) course from Switzerland to Holland.
- Dana and Donald Starkell travelled 12181 miles (19603km) by canoe from Manitoba in Canada to Belem in Brazil.

Slalom

Slalom is the most popular form of canoe competition, usually held on wild water and open to four classes. Single cockpit kayaks with double bladed paddles are known as K1M for men and K1L for women. Canadian canoes, where the competitors kneel using single bladed paddles, are known as C1 or, where there are two paddles as shown in the photo, C2.

The nature of the course means that the boats must be highly manoeuvrable. The top competition boats are made with as short a **waterline length** as possible so that they turn easily. They have low decks and minimum buoyancy so the bow or stern can be dipped under the poles of the slalom **gates,** saving precious seconds.

Slalom racers usually go through the course one at a time, but there are also team races in which three boats paddle the course at the same time. They are timed from the first starting to the last finishing, with all penalties added together.

Slalom competition

The first world championship was held in Switzerland in 1949. Since then, slalom competition has grown rapidly. Britain currently leads the world with over 5000 registered competitive slalomists. World championships are now held every year, with over 25 nations competing. Slalom is graded according to the difficulty of the water. There are six divisions ranging from the Beginners' Division 5 through Divisions 4, 3, 2 and 1 to the Premier Division. Paddlers gain experience on progressively more difficult water as they move up towards the Premier Division.

The course

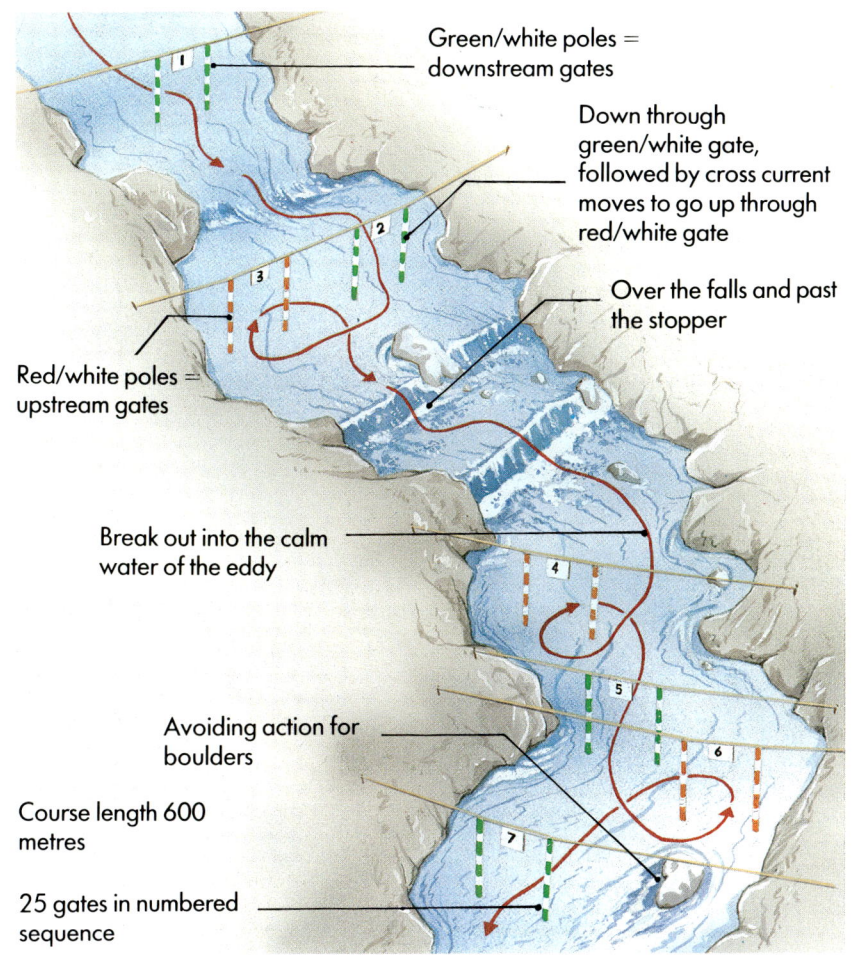

Green/white poles = downstream gates

Down through green/white gate, followed by cross current moves to go up through red/white gate

Over the falls and past the stopper

Red/white poles = upstream gates

Break out into the calm water of the eddy

Avoiding action for boulders

Course length 600 metres

25 gates in numbered sequence

The slalom course consists of a series of 20 to 25 gates, through which the paddler has to travel over a course length of 400 to 600 metres. Each gate is made up of two hanging poles set a metre apart. They are usually positioned above eddies, standing waves, or at some other tricky part of the course. Each gate is numbered and must be negotiated in sequence. Those marked red/white on the upstream side are passed to the left, and those marked green/white on the downstream side to the right. Each time a competitor hits a pole he is penalized 5 seconds. If he misses a gate or goes through in the wrong direction he's penalized 50 seconds. These penalties are added to the time taken to complete the course.

Hotdogging

Hotdogging is making your canoe perform tricks and stunts. It is mostly done for fun on wild water. Tricks include sitting sideways in stoppers, surfing while you twirl the paddle over your head or throw it in the air, turning the boat vertically on its nose or bow, and somersaulting it end over end. Hotdogging contests started to become popular in the US, and in 1991 the first World Stunt Boat Championships were held in the tidal rapids off the coast of St David's in Wales, at a spot called The Bitches. Competitors from five countries took part.

Squirt boating

Squirt boating originated in the US, using very low volume kayaks to perform hot dog style tricks in wild water. These boats are so small that they are usually custom made to fit each paddler, with just enough volume to stay partly afloat when at rest. Due to the low volume they are highly manoeuvrable when they're moving. In flat water a squirt boat can be stood on end or cartwheeled. On fast moving water it can be made to skyrocket through the air or used for stopper blasting. Stopper blasting is surfing a stopper with the bow pointing upstream. The techniques needed for squirt boating are very different from kayak paddling.

Canoe polo

Canoe polo is played by teams of five canoeists, usually in a swimming pool. The aim is to score goals, by throwing the ball into a water polo net two metres above the water. It's a fast game, which is good to watch. The players wear helmets and most also wear face cages to protect them against accidental swipes by paddles. Each half of a match lasts seven minutes. The opposing teams line up and sprint for the ball. Once a competitor has taken possession, the ball can be held for up to five seconds before being passed by throwing with the hand or flicking with the paddle. If there is a foul, or the ball goes out of play, the opposite team gets the ball. Fouls include obstructing an opponent, reaching over his boat for the ball, and dangerous use of the paddle.

Other events

In **sprint racing** long, slim, directional canoes and kayaks are raced on water that is as still as possible over 500, 1000 and 10 000 metre distances. The 500 and 1000 metre events are an established part of the Olympic Games, and World Championships for all three distances are held every odd year. The classes include one-person, two-person and four-person canoes and kayaks, racing in straight lines with no turns in the course. **Marathon racing** usually takes place over longer distances on rivers and on the open sea. Events range from a 6km Division 9 race to Britain's annual 200km Devizes to Westminster race.

Canoe cruising

A canoe cruise can be a day out on a local river, a three month long expedition to explore the wild water of Nepal or anything in between. There is something for everyone. Your first need is to get the right boat for the job.

On placid water, the faster or more racy a kayak or canoe is, the more exhilarating it will be. However, due to its longer, narrower shape it will also be considerably more unstable. Most paddlers, who have a keen sense of balance, learn to master racing boats quite quickly, while adult learners feel happier paddling a fast tourer. A kayak fitted with a rudder may be also worth considering. The rudder is operated by foot using a tiller bar. Once the basic paddling strokes have been mastered the rudder helps both steering and directional stability.

Access

In some countries access to rivers and inland waters may be restricted where the water and river banks are privately owned.

If you are challenged on a waterway, always act courteously. Never give cause for complaint by unnecessarily disturbing wildlife, fishermen or other water users, and you will most likely be allowed to paddle by unhindered.

The relevant national authorities listed on page 46 can give general information on rights of access. If in doubt you should:
● Ask permission to launch
● Ask permission to use a waterway
● Ask permission to land
● Check if you need a licence

Planning a long cruise

You need food, shelter and a suitable boat if you are going on a long cruise. On rivers with a minimum of wild water, open deck Canadian canoes have plenty of room which is easily accessible. For rougher water a kayak may be preferred, even though carrying capacity is much more limited. All stores should be packed in watertight containers and bags, and fixed securely so they won't get lost if you capsize. Heavy items should be kept away from the ends of the boat and packed so that the boat floats level. Buoyancy which is not part of the boat's structure can be removed to make more space in a kayak, but the stores should provide enough alternative buoyancy. Make sure the things you most often need come easily to hand. Remember, 'last in, first out!'

Camping

● Use a lightweight tent.
● Choose a site where you can go inland easily.
● In countries where it is required, get permission to camp.
● Make sure the boats are secure.

Sea canoeing

These kayaks crossed the Bering Strait in 1989.

Offshore sea touring can involve difficult journeys during which the paddler may be exposed to rough seas and weather. Inuit style kayaks are favoured for these kinds of trips. They must be reinforced with watertight bulkheads and fitted with pumps for removing the water. Essential equipment for offshore trips includes a spare paddle, charts, compass, and distress flares.

Inshore paddling is less demanding. Nevertheless a full understanding of wind, tide and waves is necessary. Waves are constantly moving, and require good use of sweep strokes and stern rudders. If you are swept sideways among the waves lean in and use a bracing stroke. If you are paddling in surf close to swimmers and you lose control, capsize to prevent collision.

Tides

Most seas are affected by tides. In some areas they have a dramatic effect. The tide acts in a 12 hour cycle. Low tide follows six hours after high tide. High tide follows about six hours after low tide. The tide takes half an hour to turn so that every day the times of the tides get a little later. Tide Tables show tide times at different places. A paddler must be aware of which way the tide is running and when it will change. Round a headland a tide can be very dangerous.

Waves and surf

Waves behave according to the conditions. If winds are blowing towards the shore the waves build up quickly and are closely spaced. If the winds are blowing from the shore to the sea they build up more slowly and much further out to sea. The waves are broken into surf by sandbanks, reefs, or the shore when the water depth becomes shallow. At high tide the surf can be much more violent than at low tide, as the beach is usually steeper away from the shoreline.

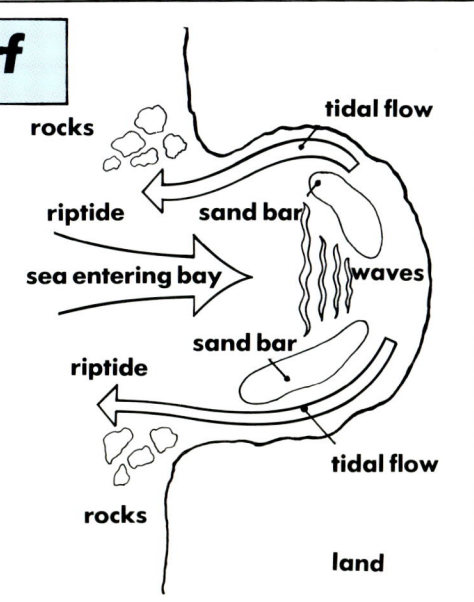

rocks

tidal flow

riptide

sand bar

sea entering bay

waves

sand bar

riptide

rocks

tidal flow

land

Surfing

Surfing events on the sea are held for kayaks and specialist surf skis. Points are awarded by judges for style, difficulty of manoeuvres and number of manoeuvres completed. Surf skis are really closer to surfboards than to conventional canoes. They are very short and very light, and have a dip in the deck forming a seat.

Safety first

● Look out for other water users.
● Beware of **dumping** waves at high tide.
● Only one boat should ride a wave at a time.

Wild water in Europe

Britain's best known locations include Grandtully in Scotland, Canolfan Tryweryn at Bala in Wales, and the artificial slalom course at the National Watersports Centre at Holme Pierrepoint, Nottingham. This was purpose built, with permanent rapids and obstacles, for year round competition.

The major rivers of the European mainland are fed from glaciers and mountains. They carry a much greater water flow than those in Britain. In the Alps and Pyrenees they are potentially more demanding, but many stretches have been spoilt for canoeists by hydroelectric development.

In France the Loire has several hundred kilometres of Grade 1 difficulty, while the Dordogne is mostly Grade 1 with some Grade 2.

The Rhone, Tarn and Ardeche all have good canoeing stretches. Germany has a number of short wild water rivers in Bavaria south of Munich. In Austria there are many wild water rivers and fine mountain scenery for all levels up to Grade 6. Switzerland has wild water ranging up to the impossible, while northern Italy has its share of steep Alpine rivers. Yugoslavia has wild water flowing through deep gorges where both access and paddling are difficult. In Spain and Portugal wild water flows from the Cantabrian Mountains, and on the Spanish side of the Pyrenees. To the north Scandinavia has many kilometres of wild water, some of it fairly uncharted.

Wild water on Austria's River Oetz.

44

The Americas and Asia

The world has so much wild water with competition possibilities that it is impossible to mention more than a few favourites. Top of the list must be the Grand Canyon of the Colorado River in the US. This flows through a 1.6km high and 1.6km wide canyon, with the Arizona and Nevada deserts on either side. The Grand Canyon also has some of the most challenging rapids in the world, and is thought to be one of the greatest wild water experiences. In the 364 kilometres (226 miles) between Lees Ferry and Diamond Creek, there are 160 sets of rapids, some dropping up to 40 metres over a short stretch. The river can be paddled in around 12 days fairly easily if you are an experienced paddler.

Elsewhere, the land surrounding the best wild water rivers may not be so highly developed as in the US. The Bio Bio, Chile's largest river, is claimed by some to be the most dangerous river in the southern

Calm waters on the lower reaches of the Indus in India, the longest of all the Himalayan rivers.

hemisphere. It starts mildly, but as it cuts west through the Andes mountains, it drops in a series of steps with increasingly severe rapids through the main canyons and gorges. These have names like Nirrecco, Quiet, and Royal Flush, and once you are in them there is no escape, except downriver towards the Pacific. The best months to canoe down the Bio Bio are January and February. One well-known trip takes about 10 days. You can camp at settlements on the way.

On the other side of the world, the Himalayan rivers of eastern Nepal offer unrivalled wild water experiences. The Dudh Kosi, Tama Kosi and Sun Kosi are three among many linked rivers in the shadow of Mount Everest. You can reach them from Kathmandu.

International associations

American Canoe Association Inc,
Suite 1900, 8580 Cinder Bed Bld,
PO Box 1190, Newington,
Virginia 22122

Australian Canoe Federation,
Room 510, Sports House,
157 Gloucester Street, Sydney,
NSW 2000

British Canoe Union,
John Dudderidge House,
Adbolton Lane, West Bridgford,
Nottingham NG2 5AS

Canadian Canoe Association,
1600 Prom James Naismith Drive,
Gloucester, Ontario KIB 5N4

French Canoe Kayak Federation,
BP58, 87 Quai de la Marne, F94340
Joinville le Pont

Italian Canoe Kayak Federation,
Viale Tiziano 70, 00196 Roma

New Zealand Canoeing Association
Inc,
PO Box 3768, Wellington

South African Canoe Federation,
PO Box 1069, 4000 Durban

Swiss Kanu-Verband,
Obere Rebgasse 19, CH-4314,
Zeiningen

Glossary

ABS plastic: a hard plastic used to make paddle blades
blow moulded polyethylene: a very durable plastic which is blown into a heated mould to make low cost kayaks
bow: front of the canoe
bow rudder: a stroke used to pull the bow sideways
break in/out: entering or leaving the main stream from/to a calm water eddy
broadside: sideways-on to the flow
buoyancy: flotation
buoyancy aid: flotation vest
buoyancy block: a lightweight, highly buoyant foam block
Canadian canoe: open canoe
closed cell foam: foam which is impervious to water
coaming: lip round the cockpit edge
cockpit: central sitting area of a kayak
directional stability: keeping the boat in a straight line

drawstroke: a stroke which draws the canoe sideways
dumping: a wave which crashes down onto a beach
edging: keeping the boat tilted
ethafoam: a soft, closed cell foam
expired air resuscitation: a first aid technique to put air back into the lungs
feather: controlling the angle of the paddle blade
ferry glide: crossing the main stream to allow for sideways drift
footrests: support bars
forward sweep stroke: a long stroke to turn the canoe forwards
gates: poles marking slalom course
gunwhale line: line round the outside of a kayak
hand roll: rolling without a paddle
HI rescue: a rescue technique in which the upturned canoe is laid across a paddle held between two other canoes

high recovery stroke: a stroke which steadies the canoe by bringing the paddle blade down flat on the water

high stroke: a stroke with the paddle held high

hip flick: a roll of the pelvis to bring a canoe out of capsize

hypothermia: a dangerous condition in which the body gets colder and colder, with the result that internal bodily functions gradually close down

inshore: by the beach

kayak: a canoe with enclosed deck

kevlar: an exotic, lightweight plastic

leading edge: the edge of the paddle blade nearest the bow

leaning: leaning with the body to help control a turn

lifejacket: a flotation jacket which gives maximum support to an unconscious person

low brace turn: leaning into a turn using the paddle blade for support

low recovery: a support stroke with the paddle held low

low stroke: a stroke with the paddle held low

marathon racing: long distance racing, usually on rivers

offshore: away from the shore

pawlata roll: a forward roll in which the hands are moved on the paddle

positive buoyancy: the amount of weight that will be supported by the buoyancy. For instance a buoyancy aid with 6kgs buoyancy will float a 6kg weight.

recovery stroke: a stroke used to recover from a potential capsize

reverse screw roll: a roll leaning backwards with the hands in a fixed position on the paddle

reverse sweep stroke: a long stroke to turn the canoe backwards

rocker line: the curve in the bottom of the boat

roto-moulded polyethylene: a very durable plastic which is rotated in a heated mould to make low cost canoes

screw roll: a roll leaning forwards with the hands in a fixed position on the paddle

sculling: moving the paddle blade back and forth through the water

sculling brace: sculling to prevent capsize

sculling draw: sculling to pull the canoe sideways

sculling for support: as for sculling brace

sideslip: the amount a boat is pushed sideways by the current

slalom: a competition involving tight turns round marker poles

spraydeck: watertight cover which fits round paddler's waist and round cockpit coaming on a kayak

sprint racing: straight line racing over flat water

stern: back of the canoe

stern rudder: a turn induced by trailing the paddle blade next to the stern and pulling it in or pushing it out

steyr roll: a reverse pawlata roll

stopper: vertically circulating water

storm roll: a deep water roll

toggles: handholds at either end of a canoe

vertical paddle roll: a roll with the paddle held vertical

volume: the internal space in a canoe

waterline length: the length of the boat in the water

white water: breaking water

wild water: more violent breaking water

X-rescue: a rescue technique in which a capsized canoe is held across another canoe

Index

The numbers in **bold** are illustrations